CAN I REALLY DO THIS

EVEN WITHOUT A DADDY

Sylvester Jones Jr.

Copyright © Sylvester Jones, Jr.

All rights reserved. Except as permitted under the United States Copyright Act of 1976, no part of this publication may be reproduced, distributed, or transmitted in any form or by any means, or stored in a database or retrieval system, without the prior written permission of Sylvester Jones, Jr.

Scripture quotations labeled KJV are from the King James Version of the Holy Bible.

Scripture quotations labeled NIV are from the Holy Bible, New International Version, NIV. Copyright © 1973, 1978, 1984, 2011, by Biblica, Inc. Used by permission of Zondervan. All rights reserved worldwide. www.zondervan.com

Edited by Eagle Eye Editing and Proofreading Services
Cover and Interior Design by MarcMaking LLC.

Special thanks to the,"W.K. Kellogg Foundation-Connecting Leaders Network Fellow" for selecting Sylvester Jones, Jr. as a Connecting Leader, 2014-2016

Dedication

The first edition of *Can I Really Do This, Even Without a Daddy?* is dedicated to my mother, Bettie Carter-Jones.

ACKNOWLEDGE-
MENTS

> In the end, we will remember not the words of our enemies, but the silence of our friends.
>
> Rev. Dr. Martin Luther King Jr. (King, n.d.a)

This quote, from Rev. Dr. Martin Luther King Jr., reminds me that doing God's work can be agonizing and lonely but that is not an excuse to avoid the assignment. When you are a child of God He will give you an assignment that is as special and unique to you as your fingerprints. Yes, each of us has unique fingerprints and we also have a unique assignment. Completing this book has taught me that we must accept our assignments in spite of the loneliness that we will experience.

Rev. Dr. Martin Luther King Jr. had an assignment. I can imagine that he was very lonely on many occasions, including his time in the Birmingham jail. In spite of his loneliness he had to accept the assignment that God had for him. I can imagine that he was disappointed by the lack of support he received from those he expected love and respect from and he was amazed and surprised by the support he received from others.

I am convinced that with God all things are possible. Because God understands that we need companionship and support on earth, He will surround us with angels and give them a special assignment — that assignment is to support you, His anointed.

I would be remiss if I did not recognize the angels God placed in my life. These angels offered the love and support necessary to complete this book and many other assignments.

First and foremost, I would like to thank my Lord and Savior, Jesus Christ, for equipping me with the knowledge and skills to complete this book. Without Him this book would not have been completed.

I would like to thank my parents for giving me life. While my father was not emotionally involved in my life, he gave me life and for that I am thankful. My mother, who gave me life and sacrificed for my sisters and me.

Next, I would like to thank my sisters, Cheryl and Camilla. I love them both immensely and they are special to me. It is important to me that they know that I love them and I am blessed to be there Big Brother (smile).

To my Big Brother and Cousin, Craig Jones. You are so much more than a cousin to me. You are my big brother and I love you. I will always remember how you guided, nurtured and protected me. Thanks for everything.

I would like to acknowledge my first cousin and friend, Jimmy Donald. Our conversations about life inspire and motivate me. The lifelong friendship we have enjoyed is important to me.

It is imperative that I acknowledge the expertise and professionalism of Danielle Ward of Eagle Eye Editing and Proofreading Services. Your commitment to producing a high-quality product is amazing. I am glad my friend Danielle Green connected me to you. I am looking forward to working with you on other projects.

I would like to thank my basketball coach, Eric Lawson, and my wrestling coach, Al Collins. Each of you believed in me when I needed you most. My children continue to benefit from the lessons and skills I learned from you. Thanks for your generosity and mentorship.

I would be remiss if I did not recognize and acknowledge special childhood friends — Xavier Brewer, Anthony Crater, Jimmy Handley, Kerry Horton, Steve Kemp, Sheldon Neeley, Sam Roberts and Curtis Steele. The time we spent together shaped who I am today. Our brotherhood and friendship has a special place in my heart.

Thank you to my college friends and fraternity brothers, Robert Bisbee, Dr. Jeffrey Boggan, Derrick Casey, John Crew, Jeffrey Fishback Antonio Hopkins (deceased), Darryl Russell, Omar Sawyer and Myron Smalls (deceased). Thanks for the memories and brotherhood.

It is impossible for you to understand how special our relationship is to me.

I would like to acknowledge special friends, Gary Jones, David McGhee and Vincent Price. You guys inspire me in your own special way. Keep doing your thing. The world needs your unique passion, skills and talent.

Pastor George Wilkinson, you are an impressive man of God. I am inspired by your generosity and passion for Jesus Christ.

Moreover, God blessed me with two amazing children — Leah and Sylvester III. You will do great things in your life and I am so blessed that God gave Julie and me the honor and privilege to be your parents. You are talented beyond measure. I am honored to be your Daddy!

Last, but not least, God blessed me with a phenomenal woman as my wife. Julie, you are the wind beneath my wings. Thanks for marrying me on September 26, 1998. I am looking forward to many, many more years of being your husband and friend. You are still the one that makes me smile!

TABLE OF CONTENTS

FOREWORDS
David R. McGhee
Rev. George Wilkinson

INTRODUCTION

1. Forgive Your Absent Father
2. Respect Your Mother
3. Resist Peer Pressure
4. Achive Academic Success
5. Avoid Criminal Behavior
6. Avoid Early Parenting
7. Develop Core Values
8. Excel In Sports
9. Serve Others
10. Afterword

REFERENCES

FORE-
WORD

Congratulations!

If you are reading this, you are preparing to do yourself a huge favor. This book will serve as a form of inspiration, but more importantly, it will serve as a source of hope. I don't know you personally, but what I do know is that the negative effect of fatherlessness knows no boundaries. I would run out of fingers if I began to count the number of individuals I know who are faced with the reality of not having a father. I'm sure you would too.

This trend is slowly becoming normal and results in unintended consequences in every corner of America. And so it begs the question, *Can I Really Do This, Even Without a Daddy?* I say, yes! Regardless of what your life experiences have been up until this point, stand firm in the fact that you are alive today for a reason. Give yourself permission to live, learn, play and be given second chances for your mistakes, past, present and future.

As you dive into this book, my hope is that you remain encouraged despite the fears you may have regarding your own life and experiences. Many refer to the world we live in today as "interdependent." This means we cannot escape each other's problems. The spread of disease, threats of school shootings and terrible terrorist attacks are things we are all vulnerable to. Yet, the issues present among males (especially African American males) are strikingly scary.

I know you are facing many challenges. It is no secret that from an early age predictions are being made about you and your peers. These are predictions of your academic ability, social competency, dropout rate, incarceration rate and so on. Yet, you are still faced with the daunting task of beating the odds as you discover what success looks like. As you live and learn every day, I want to encourage you to never lose hope.

No matter how insignificant you may feel, find confidence in the fact that someone is counting on you. Yes, it may seem that others are working hard to make sure you fail, but do know that there are also those of us who have committed our lives to making sure you succeed. No, every white police officer isn't out to kill you. But, on the other hand, every person you call your friend isn't there to help you. This is why hope is important. The decisions you make today could very well determine your destiny. I know life is hard, but even during hard times you should never lose hope.

Hope is the fuel you will need to fight through your failures and launch into your future. Let hope be your ammunition as you navigate through this world that encourages boys to remain boys as long as possible — well into their 20s and 30s — while many girls are forced to be women long before they are ready. Hope for a better day and believe one is coming. I encourage you to surround yourself with positive friends, make good use of your time and develop your character. If, at times, you don't feel accepted, take permission to accept yourself.

We are living during trying times and violence seems to be at an all-time high. I've lost friends to gun violence myself, and it is never a fun thing to experience. As an African American male, I've also been in situations where I've feared for my own life. During trying times, I too embrace hope. Death and violence are among us everywhere we look and turn, but this doesn't have to be our fate.

I may not know you personally, but if I could reach out and give you a hug right now, I would. I would offer this embrace to remind you of your importance and encourage you to hope for a future that defies what many expect from you. I'd look you square in the eyes and tell you I love you, I believe in you, and that your life matters.

Buckle up and prepare for your life to be changed for the better as a result of picking up this book.

With hope,

David McGhee
Flint, MI
www.davidmcghee.org

FORE-WORD

"All...that you see I will give you..."
Genesis 13:15

We live in the midst of turbulent times. People experience more fear, anxiety and hopelessness than ever before. At the root of many of these issues are absent fathers who inhibit maturing individuals in the home. Without key principles and practices being incorporated into the mindset of the individual who does not have an active daddy, many undeveloped and uncultivated minds will go astray. The outcomes can be extremely negative — family breakups, teen violence, crime, absence of spiritual values, lack of job security, soaring suicide statistics and a heightened risk of incarceration.

In my humble opinion *Can I Really Do This, Even Without a Daddy?* by Sylvester Jones — devoted son, loving husband, civic/ministry leader and diligent dad — provides much-needed answers for those who are in the difficult and challenging situation of growing up and living life without a focused and faithful father.

As one who lost his father due to cancer at the age of ten years old and lived my most impressionable years without a dad, I can truly relate to every chapter of this playbook for life. Many times I wondered what should I do and where should I go, and at that moment I wished I had a dad to speak with to assist me. Yes, there were surrogate dads, and yes, they made an impact, but there is no one like your earthly dad. *Can I Really Do This, Even Without a Daddy?* provides the playbook and spiritual insight to encourage and inspire you through tough times.

Sylvester Jones bases his concepts and principles on the Bible, the greatest resource for identifying one's potential and purpose to live a meaningful and successful life, even without an active daddy. He also describes his pain, mistakes and learnings as it relates to his personal journey of being able to endure the pain and rise to become an active, committed, engaged dad and leader.

Can I Really Do This, Even Without a Daddy? gives you the keys to having the authority, ability and capability given to you by God in key areas of your life to live with courage and confidence. It will give you the methods to help you navigate the arduous path of life without a daddy.

I believe that when you read the stimulating chapters titled Core Values, Forgiving Your Dad, Respecting Your Mom and Avoid Early Parenting you will come to the conclusion that with these principles you can, even without a dad. Sylvester Jones helps you recognize that you can, even with the odds against you, when you have a playbook to guide you and the Lord to lead you. Yes you can!

Can I Really Do This, Even Without a Daddy?, will be used for years to come as a bright light to lead us out of the tunnels of mediocrity, fear and despair due to being the victim of a fatherless environment.

God can do anything, you know — far more than you could ever imagine or guess or request in your wildest dreams! He does it not by pushing us around but by working within us, his Spirit deeply and gently within us (Ephesians 3:20 MSG).

Pastor George Wilkinson
Word of Life Christian Church

INTRODUCTION

What happens when you get lemons? You either eat the lemons with a frown on your face with every bite taken or you make lemonade. This work is not designed to be a panacea or a silver bullet. This work is designed to be a tool for those who have made up their minds that they will make lemonade when they are given lemons.

As I write this work I fully understand that I did not ask to be born. I didn't select my parents and I certainly never asked my father to be absent from my life. If you have an absent or deceased father, we have a lot in common. If your father is dead, you can take solace in the fact that he is not available to be in your life due to his untimely demise.

Like me, if your father is not emotionally involved in your life, this book is for you. *Can I Really Do This, Even Without A Daddy?* is designed to equip you with the tools to overcome your situation of having an absent father. The lessons and recommendations that are offered may not work for everyone; I fully understand that. I am not naïve enough to believe what worked for me will work for everyone. I am smart enough to know that there is no substitute for hard work.

If you have an absent parent, you will struggle with a negative self-concept. You will have moments of anger, moments of jealousy and you will have moments of rage. The important thing to remember is that no matter how you handle your situation — positively or negatively — your outcomes are yours. What am I saying? That is a great question. If you do the work necessary to overcome your loss, you will benefit tremendously. The moment you accept your reality, your life will begin to improve and you have the opportunity to take full advantage of the resources and people who are available to you. On the other hand, if you ignore your pain and emptiness, you will be the recipient of your bad, destructive decisions.

If you harm someone because of your absent father, your father will not serve your prison time. You will be forced to deal with your unresolved anger and pain during your prison stay. If you neglect your children because your absent parent neglected you, your children will hate you, not your absent parent.

The point I am making is to do the work necessary to resolve your anger and pain and you will reap the benefits. If you fail to do the work, you will deal with the consequences. The decision is yours. There is no substitute for hard work. The work could begin now!

At the conclusion of each chapter is a blank page for

personal notes. Take the time to reflect on the information shared. Jot down your thoughts. What are your thoughts? If something strikes a nerve, find out why. It's not important that you agree with everything I say. If you are dealing with the loss of a parent, think deeply about your feelings and what you need to do to resolve your anger, frustration or pain. Nothing will be fixed overnight, that I promise.

.1.
FORGIVE
YOUR ABSENT FATHER

"The weak can never forgive. Forgiveness is an attribute of the strong."

Mahatma Gandhi, All Men are Brothers: Autobiographical Reflections (Gandhi, n.d.a)

How do you forgive someone for hurting you? When a child is brought into the world, whose responsibility is it to care for that child? What happens if the parents fail to live up to their responsibility? If your parents do not do their job in caring for you, were you a mistake?

These are but a few of the questions a kid with an absent father may be asking himself. I can tell you that I have asked myself these questions and many more. As an adult with children, the question I continue to ask myself about my absent father is if I have forgiven him. While I believe in my heart that I have forgiven my father from being absent from my life, I am really not sure. It's an ongoing process!

Certainly, my desire is to forgive him, but when I have a mishap with my son or daughter I am forced to ask myself if I have truly forgiven him.

As I reflect on my childhood, I am reminded of the fact that my father never played catch with me. As a result, I try to play catch with my son and daughter whenever they ask. My father never attended a parent/teacher conference so I try to attend all of my children's parent/teacher conferences. My father never saw me play sports so I try to attend as many of my son's and daughter's sporting events as I can.

My son has wrestled in the past, but today he is actively involved in football, basketball and occasionally he plays baseball. My daughter is a cheerleader. As of November 2014, I have a perfect attendance record at my son's wrestling meets. He has played football for six years and I have a perfect attendance record at his football games. I have only missed two basketball games, due to work commitments, and I have a perfect attendance record at his baseball games.

As it relates to my daughter, she has been a cheerleader for four football seasons, two basketball seasons and she has cheered competitively for two seasons. I have only missed two football games in four years, however, I have missed two competitive cheer meets because my son had basketball games — my wife and I had to divide and conquer.

The point I am trying to make is that as a result of my father's absence in my life, I am trying to break the cycle. I want my children to know that I love them and I am committed to supporting them emotionally, physically, financially and in every other way.

If your father was absent from your life, if and when you have children, you have a choice to make. Will you be involved in their lives emotionally, financially, physically, etc., or will you do to them what your father did to you? I believe the choice you make will be determined by whether you have forgiven him or not.

In my opinion, there are three reasons you *must* forgive your absent father. It is important to note that you must forgive him whether he is dead or alive. To make it easy, my reasons for forgiveness are framed in the three "Ys" that are extremely important to the person you see in the mirror every day.

As you might imagine, the first "Y" is *you*! You must forgive him because it is important to how you see yourself. If you have anger, frustration or pain toward your absent father it is only hurting you. Your father has likely gone on with his life. While he may think about his actions or lack of involvement in your life, that is something he must deal with.

In order for you to be a productive human being, you must forgive him. If you are not able to forgive him on your own, seek professional help. There is nothing wrong with seeing a counselor or therapist to deal with your anger, frustration or pain. As a matter of fact, forgiving him is the most important thing you can do for your present and your future.

If you have not forgiven your absent father, you may be blaming yourself or your mother for his actions. It is important that you know you had nothing to do with his actions. Better yet, I will put it this way: you had as much to do with his actions as you have to do with the weather today.

There is nothing you can do to control the weather and there is nothing you did or did not do that determined your father's actions. Forgiving him begins with you not taking his actions personally. I have learned that I must aim to be a control freak. I can only control me so I must do everything in my power to be the best me that I can be. I hope you will take this advice.

Secondly, you must forgive your absent father because of *your friends and family*. If you have unresolved issues related to your absent father, your friends and family are likely the targets of your negative energy. This is not fair to them. They do not deserve to be victimized because your father was not present.

If you love your friends and family, it is important that you deal with your anger, frustration and pain so that you do not continue to hurt them. This one is complicated because you may not know you are lashing out at them. There may be times when you find yourself in a funky mood and you just don't want to be bothered but may not know why. The anger, frustration or pain you feel on these days may be directly related to negative emotions you have about your absent father.

You must learn to forgive him so you do not continue to hurt your friends and family. No matter how old you are, you still may have negative feelings about your absent father that you are redirecting to those closest to you. Take the time to do some self-reflection and do what is necessary to preserve the relationships you have with your friends and family. Again, they do not deserve to be the target of your anger, frustration or pain.

Finally, you must find a way to forgive your absent

father because it will impact your relationship with *your born or unborn children*. I have learned that children did not ask to be born. You did not ask your parents to give birth to you, and I am certain that your born or unborn children did not ask you to give them life.

As I stated earlier, I try very hard to be actively involved in the lives of my children. I believe being involved means being there for them emotionally, financially and physically. I have heard some men say, "My child's mother gets the child support check every week," as a reason for not being involved. On other occasions I have heard men say, "I don't see my children because me and the mother don't get along!"

In my opinion, these are both poor excuses for being an absent father. Children deserve to have a mother and a father who are actively involved in their lives. Resolving your anger, frustration and pain associated with your absent father will allow you to be actively involved in the lives of your born or unborn children. Believe me, as parents, we have a short window of time to impact the lives of our children. We cannot afford to waste time because, as my mother often told me, "I am going to raise you, because if I don't the streets will." It is important that we give our children our best selves. They deserve it and it is critical to their healthy growth and development.

I pray you understand that forgiving your absent father is important for you and those you care about the most. Let's continue to work on ourselves recognizing that becoming our best selves may begin with forgiving those who have hurt us the most. Finally, do not be afraid to seek professional help. My wife is a therapist and I maintain that she has transformed many lives by helping her clients work through circumstances they had no control over.

For more information on therapy or forgiveness, consult your pastor or the office of mental health in your community. If you are an adult with unresolved issues related to an absent parent, consult your employer for services available through the Employee Assistance Program.

Can I Really Do This, Even Without A Daddy?

CHAPTER.1.
NOTES

Can I Really Do This, Even Without A Daddy?

M.ORE.

NOTES

2.
L.O.V.E.

AND RESPECT YOUR MOTHER

"Children obey your parent(s) in the Lord,
for this is right"

Ephesians 6:1 NIV

Obeying my mother was not a problem. My mother's firm position on me was very easy to understand. Her philosophy was simply, and I quote, "I brought you in this world and I will take you out." If I didn't do what I was instructed to do no one could save me from the wrath of Bettie. When she told me to do something it was as if Jesus Christ said so Himself.

I realize that times were different in the '70s and '80s. To be honest, I would not trade anything about my upbringing. Yes, there were times when I thought my mother was the meanest person in the world. Yes, there were times when I felt as though other kids were afforded opportunities and privileges that I did not have. There were even times when I had a serious dislike for my mother for some of the things she did and the decisions she made.

While I had all of these feelings in the moment, I have absolutely no regrets about any of the things my mother did to or for me. As a productive adult, I realize my mother did the best she could and I am the person that I am today because of her wisdom.

Whenever I have an opportunity to speak to groups and the subject of my mother comes up, I tell everyone that she was and is the best decision maker I have ever met. She has foresight and wisdom that I still can't understand to this day.

She knew when I was telling a lie. She knew when the friends I picked were not good for me. She knew what she could do and what she could not do and she was not afraid to tell anyone. More importantly, she showed me what was right and what was wrong. My friends and I talk about her from time to time because she had these sayings that she used when giving firm instructions. A few of her sayings are as follows:

"First time, shame on you. The second time, shame on me." This was her way of saying you may fool her once but you will not fool her twice. Even to this day, my mother is very perceptive and has a unique way of understanding human behavior. I am sure your mother has this ability as well.

Another saying I remember my mother telling me is, "Hit me, can't fight and forget to run." This was her way of saying she will not start a fight but if you hit her, she will finish it. My mother is not a violent person but she is not a pushover. She will give anyone her last dime but she will not be a doormat. She believes in giving respect and receiving it in return. I try to live by this principle as well.

Another saying that my mother uses is, "It is better to say, 'There he was,' than to say, 'There he lies.'" What does this mean? With this saying she taught me that you have to know when to hold them, know when to fold them know when to walk away and know when to run. If you still don't get it, let me break it down this way. Her advice was, and continues to be, you can win a fistfight with one person but you may not win a fistfight with more than one. Said another way in today's society, if there is a weapon involved, don't be afraid to run. After all, if you run, you can live to see another day.

I love and respect my mother because she gave me life. She sacrificed for my sisters and me and did her best to make sure we were cared for and loved. Did she make mistakes? Absolutely. My personal philosophy is that anyone who has done anything has made mistakes. Additionally, I believe that if you have not made mistakes you have not lived. More than anything, I love and respect my mother because she was present.

When I could not trust anyone else, I could trust my mother. When everyone else was against me, my mother was with me.

My advice to the reader is to love and respect your mother as well. If your father left, she could have done the same thing but she didn't. Your mother gave you life and for that reason alone you should love and respect her.

I do realize that in today's context, "mother" can mean a lot of things. When I refer to my mother I am talking about my biological mother. For some of you, your mother is your grandmother or your foster mother or your aunt who stepped in and became your mother. Regardless of who that person is, my firm advice is to love and respect that person as your mother.

Mothers play an important role and it is equally important for us to celebrate them for the "Sheroes" that they are. My mother is my biggest Shero. Allow me to share a few other stories about her that are worth noting.

My two sisters and I all had hernias, so my mother decided to put us in the hospital at the same time to have the hernias removed. We did not have a car when I was growing up so she walked from our home to the hospital every day we were in the hospital. She would arrive when visiting hours started and she left when visiting hours were over. It was dark when she left the hospital — five to six miles from our house — but that did not stop her from staying at the hospital as long as she could and walking home alone. I am certain that your mother has done similar things or made similar sacrifices for you.

Secondly, when I was about 9 years old, while playing basketball at Forest Park, an adult male hit me in the head with a basketball. We were playing "cutthroat" and he asked me for his score. When I did not know his score, he hit me in the head with the ball. I didn't know if he was playing or not so I went home to tell my mother. My mother, a short woman in stature, went to the park to find out why this man had hit her son. The situation got pretty heated but no one was hurt. I can tell you that this man never hit me with a basketball again. I am certain that your mother has done something similar for you.

Unfortunately, I don't have special stories about my

father, because he wasn't present. Because your mother is present, I encourage you to love and respect her. Do not take your anger out on her. She does not deserve it.

If you are an adult and your mother is still alive, pick up the phone and tell her you love and respect her. If she is not alive, take a moment to meditate about her and thank God for allowing you to have such a wonderful mother.

If you are a teen and you have not respected your mother as much as you should, make a firm commitment to chart a new course today. Make a personal commitment to love and respect your mother because she deserves it. Love and respect her because she is present. She will make mistakes but she still deserves your love and respect.

Let's start a movement. Let's make sure all mothers are respected. We respect them not because they are perfect but because it's the right thing to do. Loving and respecting mothers should be a core value in all countries.

Can I Really Do This, Even Without A Daddy?

CHAPTER 2.
NOTES

Love and Respect Your Mother

M.ORE.

NOTES

3.
RESIST

PEER PRESSURE

> "You don't have to disrespect and insult others simply to hold your own ground. If you do, that shows how shaky your own position is."
>
> Red Haircrow (Haircrow, n.d.)

Some people say that learning to resist peer pressure is the most difficult thing for any young person to learn. Words cannot describe how much I disagree with that philosophy. I disagree for three major reasons.

First, I believe that peer pressure is in the eye of the beholder. As parents, we must teach our children who their peers are and who their peers are not. Age alone does not make someone your peer. At some point, we must associate our peers with our position on core values. If someone has a different value system from you do you consider him or her a peer? No. If, at the age of 45, I am teaching at a community college and there is a 45-year-old student in the class, are we peers? Chronologically, we are the same age but in that situation I am not sure I would say we are peers.

Second, decisions are made (or not made) based on the perceived win-lose proposition. For example, if you have a five-dollar bill and someone offers you a one-dollar bill for your five-dollar bill, you make the decision to trade or not based on your perception of the value of money. Most people would say that you should never trade a five-dollar bill for a one-dollar bill. I agree with that position because I understand the value of money.

If I did not understand the value of money I might make the trade and later find out I made a bad decision. In this situation, I wasn't pressured into trading the five-dollar bill for the one-dollar bill. In my opinion, my decision to trade was made out of ignorance or lack of knowledge about the value of money. In this case, if I traded a five-dollar bill for a one-dollar bill, could I later say that I was pressured into the trade? Yes, I could say that, but it would not be appropriate or correct.

Finally, think about the last time you were pressured into doing something you really did not want to do. Perhaps someone was able to convince you to do something you should not have been doing at a particular time. However, if you wanted to do it, it is unfair and dishonest to say you were pressured.

I would say that we use peer pressure as an excuse for doing something we really wanted to do in the first place but didn't have the courage to say it. (Making a decision because you are under the influence of drugs or alcohol is another story.)

Resist Peer Pressure

This is a short chapter because I believe we give peer pressure too much credit. My recommendations for resisting peer pressure are simple. Ask yourself the following questions.

1. What are my core values? It is important that decisions are aligned with your core values. If you don't know what your core values are, take the time to write them down (see Chapter 6 for more information on core values).
2. What are my goals? Decisions should be made based on alignment with your goals. If you make a decision that is inconsistent with your goals, you are setting yourself up for a setback or failure. None of us want to be considered a failure.
3. Are my current friends good for me? Friends can be a crutch. If you are not careful, you will fall into a comfort zone with friends who may not be good for you. Evaluate your friendships on a regular basis. I would suggest you consider the following questions as you evaluate your personal friendships.

> a. Are you the smartest person in your crew?
> b. Is your crew trying to do the same things you are trying to do?
> c. Is your crew challenging you to be a better person or tempting you to be a bad person?
> d. Who is the smartest person in your crew?
> e. Who is the dumbest person in your crew?
> f. Who is the weakest link and why is that person the weakest link in the crew?
> g. Who is the strongest link and why is that person the strongest link in the crew?
> h. Do you need a new crew?

It is important to note that I am not making light of the influence your environment has on you. I studied sociology and I believe your environment has a huge impact on your growth and development. On the other hand, I maintain that we must be good decision makers. Again, my mother is the best decision maker I ever met and she does not have a college degree.

When I was 2 years old, she decided to separate from my father. She moved my sisters and me from Saginaw, Mich., to Flint, Mich., because she wanted a better life for us. She assessed her relationship with my dad and decided it was not a healthy one. When she realized the relationship was not good for her she made a decision to move. While I desperately wanted to have a relationship with my father, I realize she made a very wise decision. She was not pressured to stay with my father and I love and respect her for her decision.

My mother moved to Flint with three children when she was 24 years old. She didn't have a job, she didn't have a house and she didn't have a car, but she knew what kind of life she wanted for her children.

Peer pressure is not a problem if you know what you want for your life. Think deep and hard about what you want for your life and work hard to make it a reality. Be careful to eliminate anything that is an unnecessary distraction.

In addition to unhealthy friendships, other unnecessary distractions you should be aware of include:

1. Girlfriends. Companionship is important, but be careful of toxic relationships. If your girlfriend is a drain on your time and energy, you may need to discontinue that relationship.
2. Family members. While family is important, just like friendships (your crew and your girlfriend), family members can be a distraction. The "crab in the bucket" theory is a real one. Some family members hate to see other family

members leave the nest. Many other family members are afraid of success. Finally, be careful of family members who try to make you feel bad for wanting a better life for yourself. I have heard family members say things like, "Oh, you think you are better than us!" The quick answer to that is, "No! Anything I can do, you can do too." Be careful of toxic family members who are afraid to see you do well.

3. Video games. Playing video games can be addictive. Many years ago, I made a decision to stop playing video games altogether. It was taking too much time away from my studies so I had to stop. If you enjoy playing video games for pleasure I would encourage you to develop a playing schedule. For example, maybe you should only play video games on the weekends, or perhaps you might consider only playing before going to bed. Again, my philosophy is that peer pressure is used as an excuse for doing something that you really wanted to do anyway. Are you playing video games because you lack willpower or discipline?

> Are you playing video games because it makes you feel powerful or smart? If so, call it what it is.

For those of you who are convinced that peer pressure does exist, I would offer the following advice. To resist peer pressure, develop a list of the five people who are most important to you. Think long and hard about the disappointment they would feel if you did something wrong. Think about the time and energy they invested in you. Would you want to disappoint them? Would you want them to think you did not appreciate their sacrifice? If you believe peer pressure does exist, the question is, whose pressure will you allow to influence your decisions?

Finally, consider where you want to go — regardless of whether you believe peer pressure exists or not — and who you want to be, and be intentional about making your dreams become reality. Do not allow bad habits or lack of discipline to dictate what you do and who you become. Your future is too important, so become a success because you consciously took control of your life and your decisions.

Do not give anyone control of your destiny! Become a control freak over yourself. At the end of the day, you can only control yourself and no one else.

Can I Really Do This, Even Without A Daddy?

CHAPTER 3.
NOTES

Resist Peer Pressure

MORE

NOTES

4.
ACHIEVE

ACADEMIC SUCCESS

> "Your beliefs become your thoughts,
> Your thoughts become your words,
> Your words become your actions,
> Your actions become your habits,
> Your habits become your values,
> Your values become your destiny."
>
> Mahatma Gandhi (Gandhi, n.d.b)

While attending Delta College in Saginaw, Mich., I learned an important lesson. Dr. Willie Thompson — God bless his soul — offered this quote to our psychology class: "You do best what you do most and you do most what you do best" (personal communication, 1988). Simply put, if you are good at something, it is likely because you spend a lot of time doing it.

My position on academic success is simply this:

Good students are disciplined and they have good study habits. I am willing to debate this position because most of us are born with the innate ability to be good students and to achieve high marks in the classroom. Those of us who do not do well in school do not do well because we have poor study habits.

Mahatma Gandhi stated, "Your beliefs become your thoughts, your thoughts become your words, your words become your actions, your actions become your habits, your habits become your values, your values become your destiny."

If you want to be a good student, make the decision today to be a good student. When you begin to value your performance in the classroom as much as you value your performance on the basketball court or the football field, you will become a good student. You may think I have simplified academic success; allow me to offer more background.

Elementary and middle school came very easy for me. I did above average work without very much effort. I paid attention in the classroom — for the most part. I completed my classroom assignments — for the most part — and I did my homework on most occasions. As you can see, I had questionable study habits.

My poor habits caught up with me in high school. For the first three years of high school, I did just enough to get by. Honestly, I did just enough to be eligible for athletics (football and wrestling). I ended the 11th grade with a 1.9 grade point average and I knew I had to do something different.

Going into my senior year of high school, I decided that I wanted to go to college. Prior to my senior year, going to college was an occasional thought at best. Honestly, I had a pretty good idea of what I didn't want for my life but I wasn't sure what I wanted to do with my life. I knew I didn't want to live in my mother's basement. I knew I didn't want to be a drug addict and I knew I didn't want to go to jail.

Like many of you, when I was very young, I wanted to be a professional football or basketball player. I idolized O.J. Simpson and Julius Erving. In middle school I realized that I would not be very tall so I played sports because I enjoyed them and not because I wanted to be a professional athlete.

In August 1985, I decided I needed to get things together for my final year of high school or else I would have to live on the streets as a failure. What did I do? That is a great question! I made a personal commitment to earn a 3.0 grade point average every marking period. When I decided I would earn a 3.0 grade point average, that is what I did, nothing more, nothing less. As a result of this personal commitment I made to myself, I completed my senior year of high school with a cumulative 2.0 grade point average.

The poor habits I had for the first three years of high school did absolutely nothing to help me. As I reflect on my behavior I can tell you that I had a lot of fun but I wish I had been serious about my academics. Today, I realize that simply graduating from high school is not enough.

Today, I understand that elementary school prepares you for middle school. Middle school prepares you for high school. High school prepares you for college and I was going into college unprepared because of my poor study habits.

While I had poor habits for the first three years, I

did realize that the personal commitment I made to myself during my senior year was something to build on. I was convinced that I could survive in college. Further, I was convinced that I could graduate from college and I did.

The point here is not my poor performance in high school. The point I am trying to make is that I performed fairly well when I made a personal commitment to my academics. I made a personal commitment to value high school so my behavior became consistent with my value system.

Some of you have made a commitment to athletics. If you want to be a football player, you are probably lifting weights regularly. You are likely running, eating healthy and practicing drills. For those of you who have committed to being a basketball player, you are likely working on your dribbling and ball handling on a regular basis. You are taking 300 to 400 shots a day and you are running drills with a commitment to being the best basketball player you can be. I can go on and on but I believe you get the point.

My advice for academic success is grounded and framed by the acronym B.E.S.T. My four recommendations are as follows:

B — Believe. Believe in your academic ability as much as you believe in your video game or athletic ability. If you don't believe you can be a good student you will not be a good student. Your success in the classroom begins in your head. Reflect on the quote by Gandhi. Your positive thoughts about your academic ability will translate into positive actions.

E — Excellence. If you desire to be a professional basketball player you are likely taking 300 to 400 shots a day. You are doing your best to use the proper form because you want to be an excellent shooter. You must take the same approach with your academics. Practice alone doesn't make you perfect; perfect practice makes you excellent. Make a commitment to academic excellence and you will be amazed with the results. Remember my story about my senior year of high school. If I had decided to get a 4.0 each marking period no doubt I would have achieved that goal. Make a commitment to academic excellence.

S — Start. Don't be a procrastinator. In too many cases we hold off what we can do today for tomorrow. Think about the number of times you have said, "I am going to do better next time." Make "next time" the first time. Start now to be a great student. Further, I would advise you to start referring to yourself as a good student. Believe me, just because you have never done it does not mean you cannot do it. You can only accomplish something if you start. If you never start you will never achieve. At the end of the day, you must start. Allow yourself to be surprised by academic success.

T — Tell. Tell someone you have decided to become an excellent student. If you tell someone they will hold you accountable. Accountability is so important. If you are a part of a team, your coach holds you accountable. Tell someone you want to be an academic success story and ask them to hold you accountable. Telling someone will liberate you to do what you told them about. If you have decided to become a professional basketball player, no doubt you have told others. Take the same approach with your academic success. Tell someone today!

Doing well academically begins with a personal

commitment to being a student-athlete versus an athletic student. As Mahatma Gandhi has eloquently stated, "Your values become your destiny."

When you make a personal commitment to being an academic success there is no doubt in my mind that you will do it. When you make a commitment to your success you will find yourself saying no to some things that you said yes to in the past. This is a part of the process. I tell my children often, "When you say yes to something, you must say no to something else." Say yes, today, to academic success!

CHAPTER 4.
NOTES

Can I Really Do This, Even Without A Daddy?

M.ORE.
NOTES

5.
A.V.OID

CRIMINAL BEHAVIOR

"Only 12.5% of American employers said they'd accept an application from someone with a criminal record."

(Holzer, Raphael, & Stoll, 2006)

"It takes a second to get into trouble but it could take your life or a lifetime to get out of it."

Mrs. Bessie Straham (personal communication, 1985-1986 academic year)

"It is better to say, 'There he went,' than to say, 'There he lay.'"

Bettie Jones (personal communication, 1980-1986)

While attending Northern High School in Flint, Mich., I could count on three things. First, I could count on interacting with teachers who had my best interest at heart. They cared about me and they demonstrated that through their actions. While I did not always like what they were saying to me, I knew they were sharing information that was in my best interest.

Second, I could count on being around friends who cared about me and would do anything to help me. I get a chuckle when I think about the fun times I had with my friends (Anthony Crater, Jimmy Handley, Kerry Horton, Steve Kemp, Sheldon Neeley, Samuel Roberts, Curtis Steele and many others). We had so much fun that I would go back to high school today if I knew they would be there.

Third, I could count on Mrs. Bessie Straham concluding the morning announcements by saying, "It takes a second to get into trouble but it could take your life or a lifetime to get out of it."

I graduated from high school in 1986 but I still remember her advice verbatim. She understood the importance of making good decisions and avoiding dangerous behavior.

Later in life, I was introduced to Mr. Lennex Burroughs when he served as the principal at Civic Park Elementary School in Flint. I was a young professional when I met Mr. Burroughs. He was supervising high school students who worked at Civic Park as a part of the Operation Graduation program. During a conversation with Mr. Burroughs, he said, "Young people need to think about the consequences of their decisions before they act."

The words of affirmation shared by Mrs. Bessie Straham and the conversation I had with Mr. Lennex Burroughs aligned perfectly with advice I got from my mother growing up. My mother's advice was, "It is better to say, 'There he went,' than to say, 'There he lay.'"

The advice shared by these wise individuals who

care about me is simple. They were telling me to make good decisions and to stay out of trouble. I take the advice shared by my elders very seriously. I understand that they have traveled the road I am traveling now, and they want the best for me.

As you read this chapter, it is important that you know I want the best for you. I took the time to write this book because I want the best for you. I want you to be successful, therefore I want you to make good decisions.

In addition to the other nuggets of wisdom I have shared, it is important that you understand that a felony conviction could lead to legal discrimination. If you land in the court system for a felony of any kind, it could be a barrier to attending school (high school or college), living in certain neighborhoods, playing professional sports of any kind (think about the Ray Rice situation) and securing a job in a certain field. A felony conviction could prevent you from working in education, social work, medicine or other career areas that require you to work with vulnerable populations.

Again, too many of us use the fact that we grew up without a father as an excuse for not doing our best. If you can muster up the thought to use an absent father as an excuse, then you can muster up the courage to get counseling to work through your anger, frustration or pain associated with not having a father in your life.

The advice I offer for avoiding criminal behavior has worked for me, so I believe it will work for you. Before I offer my specific advice on this subject it is important to say that anything in life worth having is worth working for. If you believe anything in life will come easy, you are mistaken.

If you want to avoid criminal behavior you must be

willing to S.C.A.L.E.: Surround yourself with positive people; Create opportunities for yourself when necessary; Allow your elders to give you advice and take it; Leave people and situations that could lead to criminal behavior; and Enlighten others in your peer group when necessary.

• S – Surround yourself with positive people. I learned years ago that I will come into contact with positive people and negative people. When I meet the acquaintance of individuals, it is important that I understand the difference between those who are positive and those who are negative. People will tell you what they want you to know but they will show you who they are through their actions. Believe what people show you and not what they tell you.

• C – Create positive opportunities for yourself. It is easy to say that things are not available for you. You must be willing to create opportunities for yourself. Create a club that does something you enjoy doing. Everything in life was started by somebody. Don't second guess or minimize your ability to be a producer. Daymond John created and produced FUBU. Somebody created Tommy Hilfiger and Polo and somebody created the hip hop groups and bands we enjoy today. Be willing to create the activities you want to be a part of.

• A – Allow your elders to give you advice. As I have stated, my mother, Mrs. Straham, Mr. Burroughs and many others poured into me. They gave me nuggets of wisdom that I hold near and dear to my heart. I am a firm believer that if someone else has learned a painful lesson I should be willing to learn from them. When I was young, I was hit by a car in front of my grandmother's house because I did not look both ways before crossing the street. God allowed me to live from that experience, so I remind my children to look both ways before crossing the street. Learning from others is important regardless of age.

•L – Leave people and situations that could lead to criminal behavior. I am a firm believer that we should be aware of our surroundings. When a situation becomes toxic or dangerous, don't be afraid to leave. My mother's advice was, "It is better to say, 'There he went,' than to say, 'There he lay.'" Leaving a situation could lead to people calling you a coward, but it will also lead to you having a clean record and your life. If someone you are with pulls out a gun, leave. If someone you are with pulls out drugs, leave. If someone tells you they are about to do something that is illegal or dangerous, leave. Believe me, it will be tough at the beginning but you will develop a reputation and a habit for making good decisions.

•E – Enlighten others in your peer group. At one point in my life, I thought I was the only one being taught to avoid dangerous or illegal activity. I tell anyone who will listen that being the son of Bettie does not make you a coward. Bettie Jones is short in stature but she has a huge heart and a lot of courage. That courage rubbed off on me, so I was never afraid to tell my friends I was leaving a situation because I was not comfortable with the activities that were taking place. As I talked with my friends about my decisions I learned they were being taught similar things by their parents, and we became allies for each other. In cases when my friends were not being taught the same things I was being taught, I became an educator for them.

While attending Delta College, my friends and I were getting out of control. We were having fun and some of our activities were against school policy. We were told that if we were involved in anything else we could be expelled from the college. I told my peer group that I would not be doing anything else. I told them that if something happened in my presence I was telling because I was not going to be expelled from the college. My friends knew I was serious, so when they were about to do something that was questionable they told me that it was time for me to leave. If and when you make your position clear, others will support you. Even if they don't agree with you, if they care about you, they will let you know when it is time for you to leave. My friends still remind me of that today. A long time ago I learned that I could not be afraid to stand on my principles.

S.C.A.L.E. is the framework I have used to avoid criminal behavior, but you might have another philosophy or framework that works for you. The key is to avoid criminal behavior, because as Mrs. Bessie Straham states, and I repeat, "It takes a second to get into trouble but it could take your life or a lifetime to get out of it." Good decisions will prevent you from entering the criminal justice system or an early grave.

CHAPTER 5.
NOTES

Can I Really Do This, Even Without A Daddy?

M.ORE.

NOTES

6.
A.V.OID

EARLY PARENTING

"Marriage is honourable in all, and the bed undefiled: but whoremongers and adulterers God will judge."

Hebrews 13:4 KJV

"Poverty is on the rise in single-mother families. More people are falling into the lowest-income group."

(Yen, 2013)

From a spiritual perspective, the Bible teaches that sex before marriage is a sin. While the Biblical teaching is clear and compelling, it has not stopped many of us from engaging in pre-marital sex. As a young man who was reared in an urban setting and someone who is well steeped in urban male behavior, I understand the pressure to have sex before marriage. To be honest, I understand the temptation to engage in sex as a recreational activity.

While I do not support free sex — particularly in today's environment — I understand there are times when you can get sex when you can't get money.

For my male readers, I understand the pressure to be a player and never get married. To be honest, I thought about it myself but being a player has never worked for me. It is important that I tell you that after years of experience, I believe it is better to marry than to burn. When I say burn, I mean burn in hell. You have heard my position on peer pressure and it has not changed. Peer pressure is used as an excuse to do something you wanted to do anyway.

Further, as a parent, I understand that most of us want our children to have more than we had. What does this mean? We want our children to have access to better schools than we had. We want our children to have access to better food than we had. We want our children to have better clothes than we had. We want our children to have better housing and safety than we had and we want our children to make better decisions than we made.

If we want our children to make better decisions than we made, we must give them exposure to activities and provide them with relevant information. There is no way around it. Several factors determine decision-making but the factors at the top of the list are core values and information.

If a young person is taught to develop and understand core values, he will make decisions that are aligned with them. For example, a core value of mine is family. Family is very important to me because my mother was a strong advocate of family. I do everything in my power to make decisions that are aligned with what is good for my family. If I believe a decision will have a negative impact on my family then I intentionally choose the decision that will not have a negative impact on my family.

I have disappointed a lot of friends and colleagues because of my commitment to family, and that is okay. A real friend will understand. There have been times when people wanted me to do some things with and for them but the activity did not align with my core value for family, so I declined the activity. Certainly, there was disappointment and ill feelings toward me but I could not go against my core values.

Another core value of mine is continuous improvement. I believe that I should be better tomorrow than I am today. I try very hard to avoid making the same mistake twice. Do I always succeed? No! I have come to accept the fact that I will make mistakes. I may even make the same mistake twice because I am human, but I will do everything in my power to be better tomorrow than I am today. I try very hard to be a lifelong learner. Being a lifelong learner requires that I read daily so I am familiar with relevant information. I encourage my children to read too, because they need information to make good decisions.

I said all of this to say it is important that young men have core values and information so that they make good decisions. As a young man who desires to be successful in life, it is important that you develop a core value related to avoiding early parenting.

If you are a teen parent, you may experience the joy of seeing your child born, but will you have the money to take good care of that child? Will you be able to accomplish your lifelong career goals while caring for that precious child? Another question you must ask yourself is, "Do I want my child to grow up in poverty?" I am certain that you do not want your child to grow up in poverty.

My position is, avoid early parenting because it will allow you to focus on your educational and career goals. Teenagers should be focused on school, sports, listening to their parents, community service, their first job and having fun with friends. A teenager should not be concerned with providing for a baby. Teenagers are not built to take care of children.

There are exceptions to this rule. If something happens to your parents and you have younger siblings, then you may have some responsibility for taking care of a younger sister or brother. On the other hand, you may have a younger brother or sister you are responsible for babysitting while your mom or dad is at work or school. These are acceptable and appropriate for a teenager, but caring for your own son or daughter is not appropriate until you have completed high school, college or trade school and have a career.

My advice is:

1. Do not engage in premarital sex. Don't have sex before you get married.
2. Do not get married until you have completed high school, college or trade school and have a career.
3. If you do not have the willpower to avoid premarital sex, use protection every time. Acceptable protection is a condom. While birth control pills may prevent pregnancy, they do not prevent sexually transmitted diseases.

Avoid Early Parenting

There is no greater joy than bringing a child into the world who you have the emotional, physical and financial means to care for. Avoid early parenting — you will not regret it!

Can I Really Do This, Even Without A Daddy?

CHAPTER 6.
NOTES

Avoid Early Parenting

MORE

NOTES

7. DEVELOP
CORE VALUES

"Core values are the guiding principles
that dictate behavior and action."
(Your Dictionary, 2015)

I have come to understand that two people can make the same decision for two very different reasons. After graduating from college I started to ask myself a series of questions because I wanted to make the right decisions for my life. The timing for my self-reflection was important because I didn't want to think too highly of myself. Questions I posed to myself and a small group of friends included:

1. Why did God create man?
2. What are we supposed to do while here on earth?
3. What is the purpose of the church?

You might be surprised to know that some people have accused me of overthinking life and others have accused me of being too deep. I am okay with either opinion of me because I know that some people live to poison the lives of others.

Consider this. During a recent meeting with my pastor, he called me "complicated." Now a few years ago I would have been bothered by his opinion of me, but today I understand that his opinion of me is his opinion and not my reality. Earlier in my life, comments like that would have prompted a lengthy self-reflection session for me. Today, as a mature adult, I realize that comments made about me have more to do with where the person making the comment is in his or her life and less about me.

I have learned not to internalize a person's opinion of me because people can be cruel and will say evil things to and about me. I have learned to be grounded in who I am, and further, that I must spend my time understanding what God says about me and what He wants me to be and do. People, regardless of the position they have created for themselves, are imperfect. Because people are imperfect — and some of them can be selfish and poisonous — you must be grounded in who you are. Being grounded in who you are begins with having well-articulated core values that drive your behavior and actions.

As the quote at the beginning of the chapter states, core values are guiding principles that dictate behavior and actions. Let me give you an example of some of the core values that you have but likely never referred to as core values.

> 1. You don't eat meat.
> 2. You don't eat vegetables.
> 3. You don't wash your face before brushing your teeth.
> 4. You don't play ball in the street.
> 5. You don't go to bed before your homework is complete.

These are guiding principles that dictate your behavior and actions. Some have said that not all core values are good. Personally, I have come to believe that core values are important and when you have them you make better decisions and when you don't, anything goes.

An instructor in college told me years ago that if you don't know where you are going any road will take you there (W. Thompson, personal communication, 1988). In my opinion, we cannot wander through life without direction. My pastor teaches that we cannot be wandering generalities, we must be meaningful specifics. I believe he is saying that there are dire consequences associated with anyone going through life without core values.

It is important that each of you take the time to develop core values that will guide your decision making so that you have laser focus. Again, you already have core values, but it is likely you have never taken the time to write them down. Writing your core values will give you an opportunity to reflect on who you are and what you stand for. Additionally, writing your core values will give you something to evaluate yourself against. After all, continuous improvement is important for all of us.

As you think about your core values I would encourage you to ask yourself the following questions to start the process:

1. What is important to me?
2. What makes me happy?
3. What makes me sad?
4. What do I want to be in life?
5. How do I want people to see me?

None of these questions are closed-ended questions — a simple answer of "Yes" or "No" will not assist you in this process. Using open-ended questions is important, because developing your guiding principles is an important process. While some areas of life are simple and mundane, other areas are complex and extremely detailed. I maintain that you must think about the answer before the question is asked. For example, consider how your core values will help you when you are presented with the following questions:

1. Do you use drugs?
2. Do you use alcohol?
3. Do you skip school?
4. Do you steal?
5. Do you lie?
6. Do you cheat?

These are simple questions that you have been or will be presented with very soon. If you have not thought about the answer to these questions, when they are presented you will not be prepared. Not being prepared could result in you doing something you will regret.

Because I believe core values are important and I want everyone to have them, I am willing to share mine with you. My core values are:

- Accountability: I am accountable to God for my actions.
- Continuous improvement: I will do my best at all times. I will strive for excellence in every area of my life.
- Dignity and respect: I will treat all people with dignity and respect.
- Family: I will make my family a priority at all times.
- Lifelong learning: I will continue to pursue opportunities to develop personally, professionally and spiritually.
- Make a difference: I was created by God to make a difference in the lives of others.
- Spirituality: My God is a spirit and I must worship Him in spirit and in truth.
- Legacy: I must leave a legacy for my children and my children's children.

Some readers will agree with my core values and others will not. Again, I am grounded and I understand that I cannot make everyone happy, so my goal is to make God happy. Now that I have shared my position on core values it's your turn.

Reflect on the following questions before developing your core values. Remember that core values are guiding principles that dictate your behavior and actions. Consider the following guiding questions as you develop your own core values

Guiding Questions:

1. What is important to me?
2. Who is important to me?
3. What makes me happy?
4. What makes me sad?
5. What do I want to be in life?
6. What was I created to do?
7. If I died today, what would I want people to say about me at my funeral?

These are just a few of the questions you should ask yourself as you develop your own core values. Remember what my college instructor told me, "If you don't know where you are going, any road will take you there." Because core values are guiding principles, your core values will determine what you do, who you do it with and how you do it. Space is provided below for you to list your core values. Enjoy the process of becoming more acquainted with yourself.

CORE VALUES

"Core values are the guiding principles that dictate behavior and action."

1. _____
2. _____
3. _____
4. _____
5. _____
6. _____
7. _____
8. _____
9. _____
10. _____
11. _____
12. _____
13. _____
14. _____
15. _____

Can I Really Do This, Even Without A Daddy?

CHAPTER 7.
NOTES

Develop Core Values

M.ORE.

NOTES

8.
EXCEL
IN SPORTS

"Once discipline is established, success will follow."

Coach Nate Brown (personal communication, November 2014)

I remember wishing my dad was around to play catch with me. I remember wishing he was in the bleachers watching me play basketball or football or wrestle, but he wasn't there.

Many years ago, I used the absence of my dad as an excuse for me not being better in sports but today I know different. While having a father in your life is important, success can be achieved if you are disciplined. Discipline can be the difference between making the basketball team and being cut. Discipline can be the difference between being selected for the travel team and being a starter. Discipline may be the most underrated quality that any athlete can have. While size, strength and speed are important, discipline is the game changer.

Student athletes must understand that they are, in fact, students first. The discipline that an athlete possesses and displays must begin at home and in the classroom.

As I have said in earlier chapters, student athletes must be respectful to their parents. Your athletic training must take a backseat to your chores at home. If you want to train for your chosen sports, make sure to complete chores at home early.

If necessary, be creative as you complete your chores. Think about how raking the leaves, shoveling snow and mowing the lawn will build upper body strength. Think about doing toe raises as you collect the garbage and the curls you will do with full garbage bags. Completing house chores will keep your mom off your back while allowing you to get a nontraditional workout in the process.

As it relates to your classroom work, most school districts have eligibility requirements. If you do not meet the eligibility requirement, you will never have an opportunity to display your athletic talent. My recommendation is that you complete all classwork while in class and complete homework as soon as you get home, if possible.

If your team practices immediately after school, plan to complete your homework as soon as practice is over. It is important that you create a schedule that will allow you to dedicate time to your academic studies on a daily basis. If you don't have homework, schedule time to go over notes from class. You want to do your best to be prepared for class just like you want to be prepared for athletics. Remember, you are a student athlete, not an athletic student.

While the majority of this chapter is dedicated to giving you advice on how to be successful in athletics, it is necessary to reinforce the importance of schoolwork and being actively involved in the upkeep of your home environment.

As it relates to success in sports, I realize that playing sports is extremely important to young men. It was important to me, so I understand that it is important to you as well.

My mentoring advice for being successful in sports is grounded in the "Four D" framework.

> D - Diet. Eat balanced meals that include fruit, vegetables and protein. Your body is a machine and it is important that you give it the fuel it needs to perform at the optimum level. Consult a trainer, dietician or physician about the proper diet for an athlete who plays your particular sport.
> D - Drills. Regular drills will allow you to improve your skills. Going to practice is not enough. Improving your foot speed will allow you to improve in every sport. Other drills that improve your upper body and lower body strength is important to your overall performance.
> D - Decision Making. Visualize yourself in certain situations on the field or court in your spare time. Think about the appropriate decision for each situation. That will help you

> make the appropriate decision when it actually happens. Appropriate decision-making will increase your playing time.
>
> D - Determination. Playing sports is more mental than physical. Your mental preparation and mental toughness will help you tremendously. Determination begins in your head and is actualized in your actions. Convince yourself that you are good. Spend a fair amount of time affirming yourself as an athlete. It will pay off.

This chapter was not a part of earlier versions of this book and that was a mistake. Sports are important to young men, so it is important they have the tools necessary to perform at a high level.

As parents, it is okay to use sports as a motivator, or carrot, to get the behavior we desire, but we can kill the spirit of our young men if we do not allow them to play sports. Additionally, it is important that you think about the mentoring your son receives from his coaches.

Parents, let the coach know about the challenges you are having with your son. If he is a good person and a good coach he will assist you with challenges in the classroom and challenges at home. Remember that powerful life lessons are learned through sports. The decision making, goal setting and work ethic developed through sports will assist your child in other areas of his life.

CHAPTER 8.
NOTES

Can I Really Do This, Even Without A Daddy?

MORE
NOTES

9.
SERVE
OTHERS

> "Everybody can be great...because anybody can serve. You don't have to have a college degree to serve. You don't have to make your subject and verb agree to serve. You only need a heart full of grace. A soul generated by love."
>
> Rev. Dr. Martin Luther King Jr. (King, n.d.b)

One of America's greatest leaders — Rev. Dr. Martin Luther King Jr. — reminds us that everybody can be great because anybody can serve. While it is true that everybody can serve, it is a lost art in this economy. The ability to serve others is one of the most underrated skills on earth.

Service to others is a selfless act that essentially says, "I am willing to put my personal interests aside — for a moment — and focus on the betterment of someone else." It does not mean you are better than someone else and it certainly does not mean the person being served is less than anyone else. Service is grounded in the idea that God has blessed me with a skill I can use to bless someone else, nothing more, nothing less.

As I dive deeper into this act of goodwill that I believe will change your life, allow me to share more background information. Some of you might claim you have never served anyone else. Others of you might say you are very familiar with service and love it. For those of you who have said you have never served anyone else, allow me to remind you of a time when you carried a bag to the car for someone. Maybe you helped someone cross a street. Maybe you ran an errand for someone. Remember how good you felt? Do you remember how important you felt because you were able to help someone else? I am willing to bet you a bag of one hundred dollar bills that the person you served appreciated your act of kindness, but did not feel as good as you did.

God has given each of us gifts and talents to share with others. The Bible reminds us that if we bury our gifts we will lose them. Remember the story in the Bible when God gave one servant 10 talents, He gave another five talents and He gave another one talent? The servant given 10 talents invested his talents and they multiplied. The servant given five talents invested his and they also multiplied. The servant given one talent buried it and God took his talent away. God was upset with the servant with one talent because he did not invest it. God has given each of us talents and therefore He expects us to use them. If we do not use our talents we will lose them.

Before you run off to serve others allow me to give you more direction. First, it is important that you accept the fact that you have talent to share. After you accept the

Serve Others

fact that you have talent to share think about that one thing you would do for free. As you think about that allow me to give you some ideas. Maybe you are proficient in history, math, reading, science or social studies. You might think about tutoring young people in that subject at your local community center, elementary school or church. Tutoring is another underrated act of service that has a huge return on investment.

Perhaps academics is not your thing, but you are a talented athlete. If you are skilled at basketball, baseball, football, volleyball and/or track and field you should volunteer to coach a little league team. You likely have no idea how much young people would enjoy having you be their coach. It is important to note that a high level of skill in athletics is not a requirement. If you enjoy the game and have the patience to work with young people you can and should coach.

Perhaps your skill or talent is talking with older people. Again, this is another underrated act of service that has a huge return on investment. Older adults love to share stories with young people. If you have the interest in learning from an older adult perhaps your act of service is visiting a convalescent home on a regular basis. It is not necessary to visit the convalescent home on a daily basis. Visiting once or twice a week for one or two hours will make a world of a difference.

My final piece of advice to you about service is really simple. If you agree to coach or tutor a young person, be committed and be consistent. Do not agree to coach and then quit on them when another offer comes along. If someone else ever disappointed you, you do not want to be on the other end of that disappointment.

These are just a few ideas for serving others. For more information on how to serve others, contact your local United Way or volunteer center. Regardless of your career interest you should consider serving others. Additionally, service to others looks very good on a college or job application. I would say, however, that padding your resume should be the last reason why you serve others.

You will find that service to others has a huge return on investment and you will develop skills that are transferrable to other areas of your life. Some of the skills you will learn and further develop while serving others are:

1. Attendance. Most organizations will require a regular schedule. Do not commit to do more than you can fulfil. If you are only available one day per week for two hours do not to commit to anything more.
2. Planning. If you are required to lead a group or team, you will be required to plan ahead. Learning to plan in a volunteer setting will allow you to develop the skill and you will be prepared to plan in a professional setting. I would say that even planning to be at a certain place at a certain time is an act of planning.
3. Problem solving. Challenges are inevitable. Learn from each and every problem that you encounter. When you understand that problems will happen you are better prepared to deal with them.
4. Punctuality. When you commit to a schedule you

must follow through — arrive and leave on time. Leaving on time is just as important as showing up on time. If you leave when you are scheduled to leave you are more likely to follow through on your commitment for a longer period of time.
5. Supervision. If you are coaching a team you are supervising others. Supervision is important because you are responsible for the young people in your care. Again, learning to supervise in a volunteer setting is transferrable to a professional setting. Don't be too hard on yourself. You will make mistakes. Learn from each and every mistake.
6. Teamwork. It has been said that "teamwork makes the dream work." Many organizations will require you to work with others. Teamwork in a volunteer setting is an excellent way to learn to work with different personalities. Working with a team can be difficult but extremely rewarding. Most professional organizations require you to work with others, so get used to it.

These are just a few of the skills that you can and will learn while serving others. Believe me when I say that service to others is rewarding for you and those you are serving. More than anything, it is important that you start. Many of us are guilty of "planning paralysis." Planning paralysis is when you spend so much time planning that you never get started doing. Do not let excellence be the enemy of good. Get started with the understanding that you will learn as you go.

Remember, God gave you talents so you can use them. If you don't use them, you will lose them. Follow the teaching of Rev. Dr. Martin Luther King Jr. and be great by serving others. Your service to others will help you overcome your own feelings of loss and emptiness. Soon you will be a professional servant and you will make God smile!

Serve Others

CHAPTER 9.
NOTES

Can I Really Do This, Even Without A Daddy?

M.ORE.

NOTES

10: AFTERWORD

COUNSELING, COACHING AND MENTORING

When I was 8 years old I jumped off a tall brick foundation in Forest Park and broke my left arm. It was a terrible break. As much as my mother loved me, she could not mend my arm back together so I went to the hospital and they reset my arm and gave me a cast that I wore for nearly two months. It was uncomfortable wearing that cast but it allowed my arm to heal and today it works just fine.

When I was 11 years old, while wrestling a friend in the grass I cut my arm on a piece of glass. It was a really deep cut. As much as my mother loved me, she could not sew my flesh back together so I went to the hospital for stitches. While at the hospital the doctor gave me a shot to dumb my arm before giving me stitches. Today, I have a scar on my left arm where the stitches were but my arm works fine and my flesh is mended back together.

Two years ago my daughter hurt her knee while attending a friend's birthday party. She and her friends were jumping and doing somersaults on a trampoline. The pain in her knee continued so we took her to the doctor and we learned that she had a torn meniscus. While my wife and I love my daughter to no end we could not repair her meniscus. Repairing the meniscus required surgery. The surgeon – with an expertise in repairing knees – removed the damaged part of her meniscus and after a few weeks she was without pain and back to her normal routines.

A few years ago, my wife and I were having trouble communicating with each other and it was causing problems in our marriage. While we are both accomplished, confident, mature adults we were having trouble hearing and listening to each other. We both value our marriage so we sought professional help in this area from a marriage counselor. As a result of a few sessions with the marriage counselor we are now able to hear and listen to each other without judgement. There are times when we relapse but we do our best to remember the tools we learned from the counselor and today we have been married for more than 16 years.

Counseling

The point I am trying to make is that there are some things that require professional help. Regardless of what you have been told about counseling and therapy there is nothing wrong with it and there is nothing wrong with you if you need counseling and/or therapy. It is important that you understand that you are not deficient or flawed just because you need counseling.

A certified counselor or therapist will help you come to terms with the absence of your father and help you develop the skills and tools necessary to manage your anger and pain. As previously stated, there are severe consequences associated with avoiding the anger and pain associated with not having your father in your life.

Afterword, Counseling, Coaching, Mentoring

Recently, a mentor of mine (Dr. Larry Young) talked with me about the importance of reclaiming your inner child. It was an important conversation that I will never forget. His position is that if a man has not had his inner child nurtured – cared for – it will stand in the way of him being a good father for his own children. Not having his inner child nurtured, reared and cared for will be a barrier to his own maturity. If you are an adult male and your father was absent from your life you are likely to have unresolved childhood needs that you will need help dealing with before you can be a selfless father to your own children. Again, you are not flawed or defective if you need counseling. Get the help that you need today so that you can be the best father, husband, brother and friend you that you can be. Contact the mental health organization in your community for help right away.

Coaching

As previously stated, I learned a lot from coaches in my life. From Frances Bentley (wrestling), Al Collins (wrestling), Elbert Hicks (basketball) and Eric Lawson (basketball) to my Big Brother/Cousin, Craig Jones, I learned valuable lessons through sports that are transferrable to other areas in my life. From these great men I learned the importance of attendance, competition, conflict resolution, hard work, perseverance, punctuality, respect, self-respect, teamwork, self-confidence, and how to win and lose with grace. They reinforced the things my mother was teaching me. It bothers me that when a parent has a problem with a child taking away sports is the first thing that comes to their mind. Coaches are passionate, youth development advocates who have the child's best interest at heart. People decide to coach for many reasons but one of the reasons is that they want young people to be successful. You will be hard pressed to find a coach who does not want a child to do well in the classroom or to be obedient to their parents. Even if the coach had challenges in his or her past they want the child to be more successful in that particular area of their life. If your mom wants to take away sports, talk with her about the relationship you have with your coach. Let her know that your coach supports her and that you are more likely to improve your behavior because of sports. Be your own advocate but it is important that you follow through on the promises that you make to your mother.

Mentoring

For nearly five years, I served as the president and chief executive officer of Big Brothers Big Sisters of Greater Flint – the premiere mentoring organization in Genesee County. It was a phenomenal experience in that I got a chance to meet mentors, from all walks of life, who understand the importance of supporting the healthy growth and development of young men and women. Mentors understand that young people who have been abandoned by a parent need unconditional friendship and support to help them navigate the challenges of growing up.

Don't be too macho to accept a mentor. The relationship could last well into your adult life and that mentor will likely help you overcome some of the most difficult challenges in your life. Even as an adult I have mentors. My mentors have helped me to overcome insurmountable challenges and their counsel and guidance is priceless. If you don't have a mentor, my question to you is, "Do you want to be successful?"

If you do not have a mentor, contact the Big Brothers

Big Sisters organization in your community right away. You will find that your anger and pain is more bearable when you have someone to help you navigate the challenges of growing up.

In closing, I need you to take responsibility for your own success. Don't be afraid to ask for help. Don't be afraid to forgive. Don't be afraid to ask for a hug. Don't be afraid to say you are scared. Don't be afraid to apologize if you make a mistake. Learn from your mistakes. Growing up without a father is hard work but you can do it with the help of others in your community. Reading this book is just the beginning of your journey.

As you move forward, adopt my Ten Commandments for youth growing up without a father:

1. Apologize when you make a mistake. We all make mistakes.
2. Ask for help. We all need help.
3. Ask for a counselor. A certified counselor will help you work through your anger.
4. Ask a mentor. A mentor will offer unconditional friendship and support.
5. Develop Core Values. You must be clear about what you stand for.
6. Don't be afraid to cry. Crying is therapeutic and will help you work through anger.
7. Forgive your absent father. If he knew better, he would do better.
8. Give back to your community. Seving others will help you develop transferrable skills.
9. Work hard in the classroom. Doing well in school is critical to your success.
10. Respect your mother. She deserves your unconditional love and respect.

The answer to the question is, YES! You can do this, even without a daddy!

Can I Really Do This, Even Without A Daddy?

NOTES

Afterword, Counseling, Coaching, Mentoring

NOTES

Can I Really Do This, Even Without A Daddy?

NOTES

Afterword, Counseling, Coaching, Mentoring

NOTES

References

Examples of Core Values. (n.d.). Retrieved February 27, 2015, from http://examples.yourdictionary.com/examples-of-core-values.html

Holzer, H. J., Raphael, S., & Stoll, M. A. (2006). Perceived Criminality, Criminal Background Checks, and the Racial Hiring Practices of Employers. The Journal of Law and Economics 49(2), 451, 453–454. http://www.nij.gov/journals/270/pages/criminal-records.aspx

Martin Luther King Jr. (n.d.a). BrainyQuote.com. Retrieved November 2014, from http://www.brainyquote.com/quotes/authors/m/martin_luther_king_jr.html

Martin Luther King Jr. (n.d.b). Goodreads.com. Retrieved February 27, 2015 from http://www.goodreads.com/author/quotes/23924.Martin_Luther_King_Jr_

Mahatma Gandhi (n.d.a). BrainyQuote.com. Retrieved February 27, 2015 from http://www.brainyquote.com/quotes/quotes/m/mahatmagan121411.html

Mahatma Gandhi (n.d.b). Goodreads.com. Retrieved February 27, 2015 from http://www.goodreads.com/quotes/50584-your-beliefs-become-your-thoughts-your-thoughts-become-your-words

Miranda Rights (2015). Mirandawarning.com. Retrieved February 2, 2015 from http://www.mirandawarning.org/whatareyourmirandarights.html

Red Haircrow (n.d.). Goodreads.com. Retrieved February 27, 2015 from http://www.goodreads.com/quotes/293897-you-don-t-have-to-disrespect-and-insult-others-simply-to

Yen. H. (2013, September 19). 4.1 million single-mother families are living in poverty: Census. Huffington Post. Retrieved February 27, 2015 from http://www.huffingtonpost.com/2013/09/19/single-mother-poverty_n_3953047.html

Order Form

Can I Really Do This, Even Without A Daddy?

For additional copies of "Can I Really Do This, Even Without A Daddy?" contact Sylvester Jones, Jr. at **sjones67@comcast.net** or send this completed order form to:

Email this form to:
Sylvester Jones, Jr.
sjones67@comcast.net

Please Print:
Name of Individual, Organization or
School: _____

Address: _____

City: _____ **State:** _____ **Zip Code:** _____

Daytime Telephone Number: _____

Evening Telephone Number: _____

Email Address: _____

Credit Cards Accepted!

_____ **American Express**   _____ **MasterCard**

_____ **Discover**   _____ **Visa**

Credit Card Number: _____

Expiration Date: _____ **Security Code:** _____

Quantity: _____ x $15.00 per copy   **Total:** _____

About The Author

Sylvester Jones Jr. is a passionate advocate for marginalized youth. He has a unique ability to connect with people from different walks of life but, more than that, he is a bold, God-fearing leader who lives his faith through his roles as husband, father, brother, coach, mentor, teacher, trainer and speaker.

Sylvester is a captivating speaker and trainer who is not afraid to share the challenges of growing up without a daddy, and he has a proven track record of helping others develop the skills and resilience to overcome similar circumstances.

Sylvester is a graduate of Flint Northern High School and he has earned college degrees from Delta College, Saginaw Valley State University and Central Michigan University. He is an accomplished youth development professional who uses his education and professional experience to create sustainable, transformational change.

A 1990 initiate of Kappa Alpha Psi Fraternity, Incorporated (Xi Iota Chapter), he promotes achievement, brotherhood, fellowship and service. When not with his family and friends he can be found serving others in some capacity.

Sylvester is married to Julie and they have two children, Leah and Sylvester III. The family worships at Word of Life Christian Church and they are committed to being believing believers.

Made in the USA
Columbia, SC
02 April 2020

90248442R00063